Black Bass and Trout Fishing in the United States

Addendum to the 2001 National Survey of Fishing, Hunting, and Wildlife-Associated Recreation

Report 2001-10

I0450412

July 2005

Jerry Leonard
Division of Federal Assistance
U.S. Fish and Wildlife Service
Arlington, VA

This report is intended to complement the National and State Reports for the 2001 National Survey of Fishing, Hunting and Wildlife-Associated Recreation. The conclusions in this report are the author's and do not represent official positions of the U.S. Fish and Wildlife Service.

The author thanks Sylvia Cabrera, Richard Aiken, and Dave Buschena for valuable input into this report.

Contents

Introduction

In the movie Field of Dreams James Earl Jones says, "The one constant through all the years has been baseball. America has rolled by like an army of steamrollers. It's been erased like a blackboard, rebuilt, and erased again. But baseball has marked the time. " While it is true that baseball has withstood the test of time, it is not the only thing to have done so; fishing has also persevered. Former president Hebert Hoover once said, "Fishing is much more than fish. It is the great occasion when we may return to the fine simplicity of our forefathers." Even today, despite the multitudes of gadgets and games that all vie for attention in this electro-techno age, several recent polls indicate that fishing trails only reading, TV watching, and spending time with family as Americans' favorite leisure activity.[1]

In 2001, 34.1 million U.S. residents over 15 years old participated in fishing, and they fished a total of 557 million days. To put the total of 34.1 million anglers is perspective, one should consider the following: in 2000 there were 37.5 million families in the U.S. with children under 18.[2] This 37.5 million includes all single and two parent families and all those families with children that are not their own due to adoption, etc. There are nearly as many anglers over 15 in the U.S. as there are families with children under 18! When one considers all the families that he or she encounters at grocery stores, malls, movies, and restaurants, the total number of anglers seems astounding.

Moreover, fishing is not only important as a leisure activity but also as a catalyst for economic growth. In 2001 anglers spent a total of $41.5 billion on fishing trips and equipment, and this $41.5 billion generated an estimated $116.1 billion in economic output.[3]

Luther Goldman/USFWS

Two of the most prominent species of fish sought by anglers are black bass and trout. Black bass includes all largemouth, smallmouth, and spotted bass. Of all anglers who fished in freshwater other than the Great Lakes in 2001, 38% sought black bass and 28% sought trout. Additionally, the average spending of both black bass and trout anglers on fishing trips and equipment was notably higher than that of all freshwater anglers.

This report seeks to broaden the understanding of anglers for these two highly desired freshwater species. It provides information on participation levels, socioeconomic characteristics, expenditures, and boating usage of both black bass and trout anglers. It is intended to be used as an informational tool by resource managers, academics, product manufacturers, and other interested parties. This report focuses on freshwater fishing that does not occur

in the Great Lakes, which is consistent with prior black bass and trout fishing reports published by the U.S. Fish and Wildlife Service. Unlike previous reports, however, this report includes a short section on the number of Great Lakes' black bass and trout anglers.

For the sake of brevity, this report employs the following definitions. Great Lakes fishing is considered a distinct type of fishing rather than "freshwater fishing." This distinction permits

---

[1] Harris Polls 1994–2004. Fishing follows only these three activities in five out of the last nine years.

[2] "Statistical Abstract of the United States 2004–2005," *U.S. Census Bureau.* 2004

[3] "Sportfishing in America," *American Sportfishing Association* 2002.

references to "freshwater fishing that does not occur in the Great Lakes" to be shortened to "freshwater fishing." Great Lakes fishing is addressed separately. This report refers to black bass simply as bass, and it excludes all other forms of bass such as white bass, striped bass, and striped bass hybrids. This report excludes all boating activity for purposes other than fishing. Anglers may participate in recreational boating for purposes other than fishing, such as pleasure boating and sightseeing; however, this activity is not included in days of boating in this report. Anglers who are considered boaters are those who fish from a boat regardless of their use of boats for purposes other than fishing.

Report Organization

The report is organized into four parts:

Part One: The "Participation in Black Bass and Trout Fishing" section examines the populations and geographic dispersion of both types of anglers. Estimates of total participation levels and days of participation are made at national and state levels.

Part Two: The "Socioeconomic Characteristics" section examines the socioeconomic characteristics of all freshwater, black bass, and trout anglers. Comparisons are made among the different groups to promote a better understanding of their unique features.

Part Three: The "Expenditures" section provides a detailed analysis of spending by all freshwater, black bass, and trout anglers. Total and average spending are calculated for numerous trip and equipment categories.

Part Four: The "Boat Usage" section examines the use of boats for fishing among all freshwater, black bass, and trout anglers. Socioeconomic characteristics of those anglers who use boats are examined in detail.

Part Five: Lastly, the "Fishing by Boat Model" section summarizes the results of a continuation ratio regression model used to examine the impact that numerous variables have on the probability that anglers will participate in *some boating* as opposed to *no boating*. Additionally, the model is used to examine what impact the same variables have on the probability that an individual will participate in *avid boating* given that he or she participates in *some boating*.

All reported data contained herein are from the *2001 National Survey of Fishing, Hunting, and Wildlife-Associated Recreation (FHWAR)*.[4] Consequently, all participation, expenditures, and hunting behavior statistics are representative of 2001. Additionally, all data represents persons age 16 years and older.

---

[4] FHWAR documents are available on the U.S. Fish and Wildlife Service webpage: http://federalaid.fws.gov/surveys/surveys.html.

Part One—Participation in Black Bass and Trout Fishing

Participation Nationally

Freshwater

Table 1 reveals the number of anglers, days of fishing, and average days of fishing for different freshwater species. Additionally, the percent columns indicate the share of total anglers and days of fishing that are attributable to each species. The percents do not sum to 100 because many anglers fish for multiple species.

From the perspective of both the number of anglers and days of fishing, black bass are the most pursued freshwater fish species. Table 1 indicates that there were 10.7 million black bass anglers in 2001, which is 35% more anglers than the species with the second most anglers, panfish. These 10.7 million anglers fished for bass nearly 160 million days. The average number of days that a bass angler fishes for bass is 15 days. Walleye and sauger are the only other species sought for an average of 15 days.

Trout fishing ranks third in popularity by number of freshwater anglers. 7.8 million trout anglers fished 83 million days, which averages 11 days per angler. 11 days is lower than the majority of other species. This lower average days of fishing may be the result of relatively short fishing seasons for trout, as well as terrain, accessibility, and climate of trout habitat.

Table 1. Freshwater Anglers and Days of Fishing by Species Type: 2001

(Population 16 years of age and older. Numbers in thousands. Excludes Great Lakes fishing.)

	Anglers		Days of fishing		Average days
	Number	*Percent*	*Number*	*Percent*	*per angler*
Total, all types of fish	27,913	100%	443,247	100%	16
Black bass (largemouth, smallmouth, etc.)	10,708	38%	159,847	36%	15
White bass, striped bass, and striped hybrids	4,946	18%	61,889	14%	13
Panfish	7,910	28%	103,294	23%	13
Crappie	6,657	24%	95,109	21%	14
Catfish and bullheads	7,517	27%	103,664	23%	14
Walleye and Sauger	3,269	12%	48,514	11%	15
Northern pike, pickerel, muskie	2,060	7%	27,290	6%	13
Trout	7,819	28%	83,325	19%	11
Salmon	1,369	5%	15,053	3%	11
Steelhead	536	2%	6,698	2%	12
Anything	4,741	17%	46,257	10%	10
Another type of freshwater fish	1,537	6%	17,277	4%	11

Note: Detail does not add to total because of multiple responses

Table 2 presents the distribution of black bass and trout anglers by geographic region of the country. Additionally, it indicates the percent of freshwater anglers who were bass and trout anglers. The region with the highest number of bass anglers is the South Atlantic with 2.2 million, and the region with the highest percent of bass anglers is the East South Central with 50%. In several other regions, more than 40% of freshwater anglers pursued bass. The Mountain and Pacific regions have substantially lower percentages at around 20%. However, the Mountain and Pacific regions have the highest quantity and percent of trout anglers. Combined these two regions comprise more than half of all trout anglers. Figure 1 shows a map of the different regions along with their respective percentages of freshwater anglers who seek bass and trout.

Great Lakes
There is some bass and trout fishing in the Great Lakes. In 2001, 589 thousand anglers pursued bass a total of 6.4 million days in the Great Lakes (Table 3). In the Great Lakes bass are the second most popular species behind perch. There are roughly the same number of trout anglers fishing in the Great Lakes as bass anglers, 585 thousand. These anglers sought trout for 6.0 million days, which is also similar to the number of days bass were pursued.

Table 2. Regional Residence of All Freshwater, Black Bass, and Trout Anglers: 2001
(Population 16 years of age and older. Numbers in thousands. Excludes Great Lakes fishing.)

| Region | All Freshwater Anglers | | Black Bass Anglers | | | Trout Anglers | | |
	Number	Percent	Number	Percent	Percent of Freshwater	Number	Percent	Percent of Freshwater
U.S. Total	27,913	100%	10,708	100%	38%	7,819	100%	28%
New England	1,030	4%	463	4%	45%	566	7%	55%
Middle Atlantic	2,113	8%	990	9%	47%	1,017	13%	48%
East North Central	4,790	17%	1,956	18%	41%	517	7%	11%
West North Central	3,749	13%	1,221	11%	33%	364	5%	10%
South Atlantic	4,629	17%	2,164	20%	47%	729	9%	16%
East South Central	2,356	8%	1,171	11%	50%	214	3%	9%
West South Central	3,661	13%	1,661	16%	45%	500	6%	14%
Mountain	2,393	9%	427	4%	18%	1,873	24%	78%
Pacific	3,193	11%	655	6%	21%	2,040	26%	64%

Figure 1. Percent of Freshwater Anglers Who Seek Trout and Bass in the Bureau of Census Regions

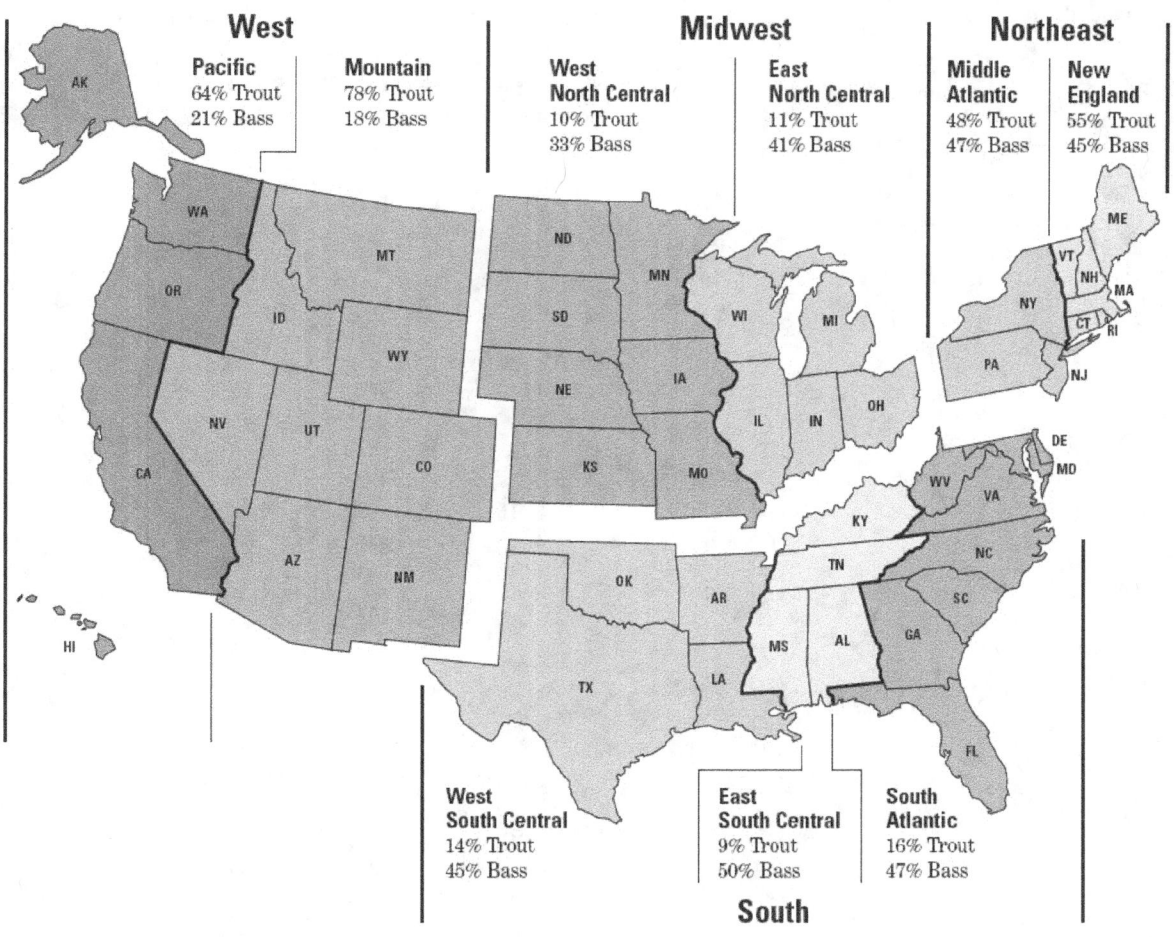

West

Pacific
64% Trout
21% Bass

Mountain
78% Trout
18% Bass

Midwest

West North Central
10% Trout
33% Bass

East North Central
11% Trout
41% Bass

Northeast

Middle Atlantic
48% Trout
47% Bass

New England
55% Trout
45% Bass

West South Central
14% Trout
45% Bass

East South Central
9% Trout
50% Bass

South Atlantic
16% Trout
47% Bass

South

Table 3. Great Lakes Anglers and Days of Fishing by Species Type: 2001
(Population 16 years of age and older. Numbers in thousands.)

	Anglers		Days of fishing		Average days per angler
	Number	*Percent*	*Number*	*Percent*	
Total, all types of fish	1,847	100%	23,138	100%	13
Black bass (largemouth, smallmouth, etc.)	589	32%	6,355	27%	11
Walleye and Sauger	571	31%	5,521	24%	10
Northern pike, pickerel, muskie	140	8%	**	**	**
Perch	693	38%	6,597	29%	10
Salmon	516	28%	3,985	17%	8
Steelhead	338	18%	3,698	16%	11
Trout	585	32%	5,960	26%	10
Anything	217	12%	1,994	9%	9
Another type of Great Lakes fish	157	9%	1,769	8%	11

Note: Detail does not add to total because of multiple responses
**Sample size too small to report data reliably.

Black Bass and Trout Participation by State where Fishing Occurs

Table 4 presents the number of freshwater, black bass, and trout anglers by state where fishing occurred. Additionally, the percent columns indicate the share of all freshwater anglers who are bass and trout anglers respectively. There is a wide variation in the proportion of anglers who seek bass and trout by state. The wide variations are attributable to differences in freshwater habit, which often favor one species over the other.

Table 4. Freshwater, Black Bass, and Trout Anglers by State Where Fishing Occurred: 2001

(Population 16 years of age and older. Numbers in thousands. Excludes Great Lakes fishing.)

	All Freshwater	Black Bass Anglers Number	Black Bass Anglers Percent	Trout Anglers Number	Trout Anglers Percent
U.S. Total	27,913	10,708	38%	7,819	28%
AK	266	**	**	83	31%
AL	732	383	52%	*19	*2%
AR	782	318	41%	131	17%
AZ	419	148	35%	219	52%
CA	1,865	495	27%	1,174	63%
CO	915	*71	*8%	806	88%
CT	255	112	44%	118	46%
DE	73	28	38%	*11	*15%
FL	1,316	647	49%	**	**
GA	1,017	389	38%	108	11%
HI	*12	**	**	**	**
IA	542	192	36%	*48	*9%
ID	416	53	13%	332	80%
IL	1,060	386	36%	*58	*5%
IN	746	353	47%	**	**
KS	404	170	42%	*18	*4%
KY	780	339	44%	*41	*5%
LA	659	273	41%	**	**
MA	325	155	48%	133	41%
MD	367	155	42%	101	28%
ME	272	107	39%	163	60%
MI	980	316	32%	177	18%
MN	1,560	343	22%	*64	*4%
MO	1,215	574	47%	195	16%
MS	494	239	48%	**	**
MT	349	*22	*6%	293	84%
NC	848	375	44%	173	20%
ND	179	*6	*3%	*6	*3%
NE	296	108	36%	*25	*9%
NH	221	97	44%	121	55%
NJ	331	171	52%	140	42%
NM	314	*47	*15%	210	67%
NV	172	37	21%	111	65%
NY	901	387	43%	321	36%
OH	1,081	494	46%	*76	*7%
OK	774	381	49%	*59	*8%
OR	611	63	10%	417	68%
PA	1,163	548	47%	646	56%
RI	51	23	45%	22	43%
SC	591	285	48%	*49	*8%
SD	214	22	10%	*16	*7%
TN	903	461	51%	137	15%
TX	1,842	892	48%	*140	*8%
UT	517	68	13%	431	83%
VA	721	390	54%	116	16%
VT	171	41	24%	100	58%
WA	659	102	15%	436	66%
WI	1,307	494	38%	115	9%
WV	318	143	45%	112	35%
WY	293	**	**	256	88%

*Estimate based on small sample size.
**Sample size too small to report data reliably.

At 54% Virginia has the highest percent of bass anglers. In Alabama, New Jersey, and Tennessee, greater than 50% of anglers seek bass. Among those states with the lowest percentages are North Dakota, Montana, and Colorado, which all have less than 10%. The survey sample sizes are too small to report reliable estimates for Alaska, Wyoming, and Hawaii. Figure 2 displays a graphical representation of bass angler share of freshwater anglers.

Many of the states with the lowest percentages of bass anglers are among the highest in percent of trout anglers. More than 80% of freshwater anglers pursued trout in Wyoming, Montana, and Colorado. Conversely, less than 5% did so in Kansas, Minnesota, North Dakota, and Alabama. The survey sample sizes are too small to reliably report the percent of trout anglers in Hawaii, Indiana, Florida, Mississippi, and Louisiana. Figure 3 displays a graphical representation of the trout angler share of freshwater anglers.

Figure 2. Percent of Freshwater Anglers Who Sought Black Bass

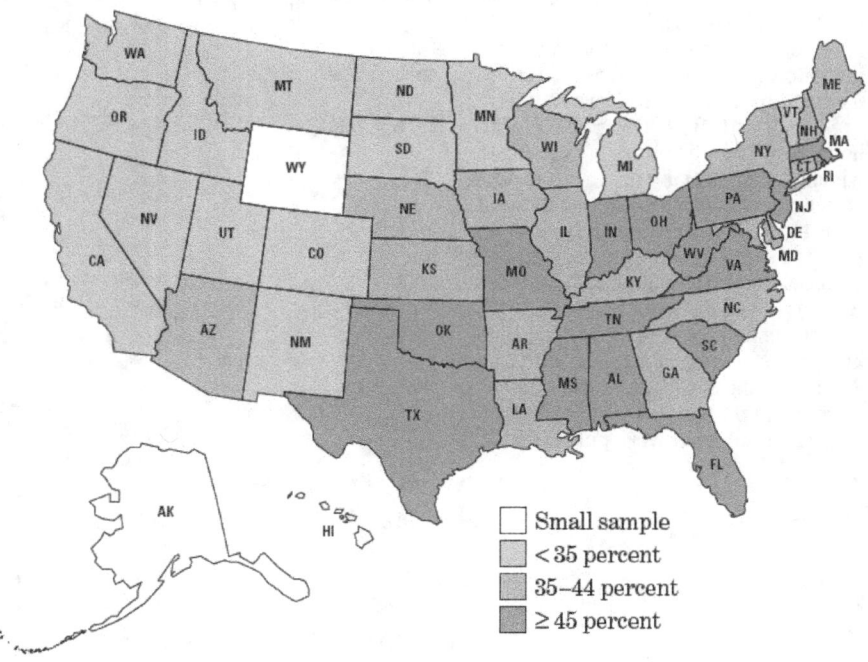

Figure 3. Percent of Freshwater Anglers Who Sought Trout

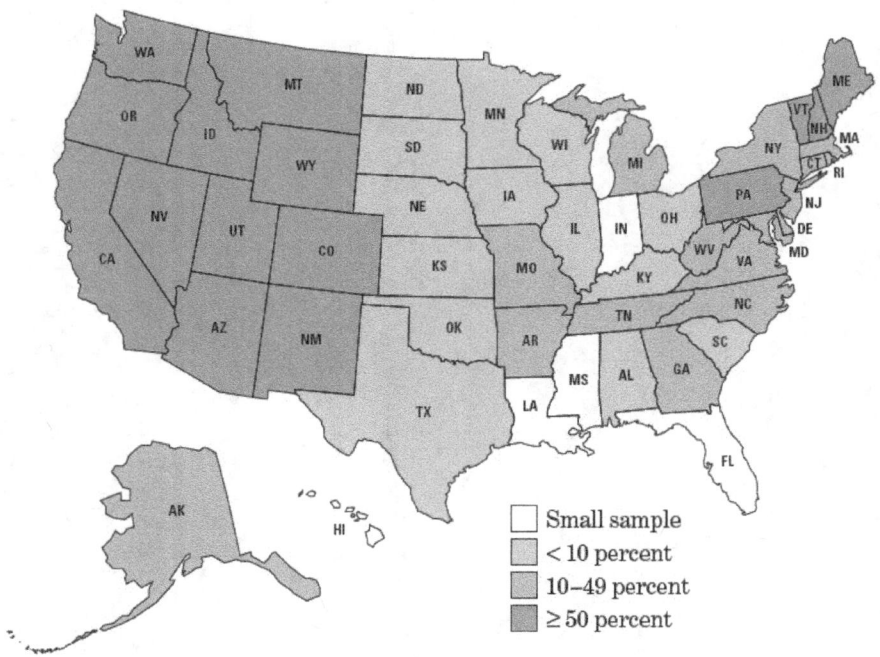

Table 5 presents the total days of fishing for freshwater, black bass, and trout by state where fishing occurred. Additionally, the percent columns indicate the share of all freshwater fishing days in which anglers sought bass and trout. Both Texas and Florida have over 12 million days of bass fishing, which is substantially higher than other states. States with the highest percent of freshwater days in which bass were pursued include New Jersey, Florida, and Massachusetts with 62%, 59%, and 59% respectively. California has the most days of trout fishing at 9.9 million. Colorado and Pennsylvania both follow with around 7.5 million days. Colorado and Wyoming have the highest percent of freshwater days in which trout were pursued at 82%.

Table 5. Freshwater, Black Bass, and Trout Days of Fishing by State Where Fishing Occurred: 2001

(Population 16 years of age and older. Numbers in thousands. Excludes Great Lakes fishing.)

	All Freshwater Days	Black Bass Days		Trout Days	
		Number	Percent	Number	Percent
U.S. Total	443,247	159,847	100%	83,325	100%
AK	2,110	**	**	605	29%
AL	9,877	5,578	56%	*154	*2%
AR	13,006	4,841	37%	727	6%
AZ	4,246	1,372	32%	1,661	39%
CA	19,385	4,121	21%	9,901	51%
CO	9,267	*864	*9%	7,637	82%
CT	3,516	1,576	45%	1,555	44%
DE	609	229	38%	*67	*11%
FL	20,840	12,215	59%	**	**
GA	13,076	4,434	34%	962	7%
HI	*194	**	**	**	**
IA	7,485	2,552	34%	*484	*6%
ID	4,070	526	13%	2,434	60%
IL	14,246	4,491	32%	*1,188	*8%
IN	12,756	6,192	49%	**	**
KS	5,662	2,395	42%	*232	*4%
KY	12,394	5,160	42%	*261	*2%
LA	8,419	2,997	36%	**	**
MA	4,560	2,670	59%	1,727	38%
MD	4,269	2,281	53%	982	23%
ME	3,422	1,275	37%	1,777	52%
MI	12,817	2,641	21%	1,356	11%
MN	28,159	4,235	15%	*834	*3%
MO	13,279	5,550	42%	1,186	9%
MS	8,466	2,886	34%	**	**
MT	4,068	*394	*10%	2,957	73%
NC	12,073	4,619	38%	961	8%
ND	2,186	*71	*3%	*40	*2%
NE	3,204	1,073	33%	*141	*4%
NH	2,871	1,084	38%	1,276	44%
NJ	5,553	3,453	62%	1,519	27%
NM	2,485	*279	*11%	1,788	72%
NV	1,575	250	16%	1,068	68%
NY	13,022	5,021	39%	3,396	26%
OH	15,212	8,705	57%	*761	*5%
OK	12,741	5,976	47%	*325	*3%
OR	7,895	541	7%	4,077	52%
PA	17,201	6,955	40%	7,263	42%
RI	649	233	36%	273	42%
SC	8,713	4,217	48%	*423	*5%
SD	2,984	245	8%	*147	*5%
TN	15,035	7,250	48%	1,785	12%
TX	25,650	12,315	48%	*824	*3%
UT	5,238	629	12%	3,899	74%
VA	10,847	5,139	47%	1,677	15%
VT	2,321	381	16%	1,305	56%
WA	9,800	1,393	14%	5,340	54%
WI	19,139	6,765	35%	1,521	8%
WV	4,152	1,757	42%	1,340	32%
WY	2,497	**	**	2,054	82%

*Estimate based on small sample size.
**Sample size too small to report data reliably.

Table 6 presents the average days of fishing for all freshwater species, black bass, and trout. New Jersey, Florida, and Indiana have the highest average days of bass angling. Illinois and Virginia have the highest average days of trout angling.

Table 6. Average Days Freshwater, Black Bass, and Trout Fishing by State Where Fishing Occurred: 2001
(Population 16 years of age and older. Excludes Great Lakes fishing.)

	All Freshwater	Black Bass	Trout
U.S. Total	16	15	11
AK	8	**	7
AL	14	15	*8
AR	17	16	6
AZ	10	9	8
CA	11	8	9
CO	10	*12	10
CT	14	14	13
DE	9	8	*6
FL	16	19	**
GA	13	12	9
HI	*17	**	**
IA	14	13	*10
ID	10	10	7
IL	14	12	*22
IN	17	18	**
KS	14	14	*13
KY	16	15	*6
LA	13	11	**
MA	14	18	14
MD	12	15	10
ME	13	12	11
MI	14	9	8
MN	18	13	*13
MO	11	10	6
MS	17	12	**
MT	12	*18	10
NC	14	12	6
ND	13	*12	*7
NE	11	10	*6
NH	13	11	11
NJ	17	20	11
NM	8	*6	9
NV	9	7	10
NY	15	13	11
OH	14	18	*10
OK	17	16	*6
OR	13	9	10
PA	15	13	11
RI	13	10	13
SC	15	15	*9
SD	14	12	*9
TN	17	16	13
TX	14	14	*6
UT	10	9	9
VA	15	13	14
VT	14	9	13
WA	15	14	12
WI	15	14	13
WV	13	13	12
WY	9	**	8

*Estimate based on small sample size.
**Sample size too small to report data reliably.

Part Two—Socioeconomic Characteristics

This section provides a detailed analysis of the socioeconomic characteristics of all freshwater, bass, and trout anglers. The socioeconomic characteristics addressed include age, gender, education, and income.

Age
The "Percent" columns for all freshwater, black bass, and trout anglers in Table 7 reveal a very similar distribution by age. The greatest percent of all three different angler types is 35–44. The lowest percent of all three occurs for ages 16–17.

Table 7. Age Distribution of Freshwater, Black Bass, and Trout Anglers: 2001
(Population 16 years of age and older. Numbers in thousands. Excludes Great Lakes fishing.)

Age	All Freshwater Anglers		Black Bass Anglers			Trout Anglers		
	Number	Percent	Number	Percent	Percent of Freshwater	Number	Percent	Percent of Freshwater
U.S. Total	27,913	100%	10,708	100%	38%	7,819	100%	28%
16–17	1,146	4%	500	5%	44%	350	4%	31%
18–24	2,576	9%	1,056	10%	41%	663	8%	26%
25–34	5,452	20%	2,200	21%	40%	1,540	20%	28%
35–44	7,492	27%	2,979	28%	40%	2,261	29%	30%
45–54	5,469	20%	2,005	19%	37%	1,564	20%	29%
55–64	3,310	12%	1,171	11%	35%	798	10%	24%
65+	2,469	9%	797	7%	32%	643	8%	26%

Gender
Figure 4 indicates that both black bass and trout anglers have a higher concentration of males than all freshwater anglers. 80% of bass anglers and 78% of trout anglers are male, which compares to 74% of all freshwater anglers. There is a higher concentration of females among anglers who pursue other freshwater species including panfish, catfish, or any freshwater fish (which indicates pursuit of no particular species).

Education
Figure 5 indicates that trout anglers are slightly more likely to have four or more years of college than all freshwater or trout anglers. 30% of trout anglers have four or more years of college, which compares to 26% of both bass anglers and all freshwater anglers.

Figure 4. Gender Distribution of Freshwater, Black Bass, and Trout Anglers: 2001
(Population 16 years of age and older. Excludes Great Lakes fishing.)

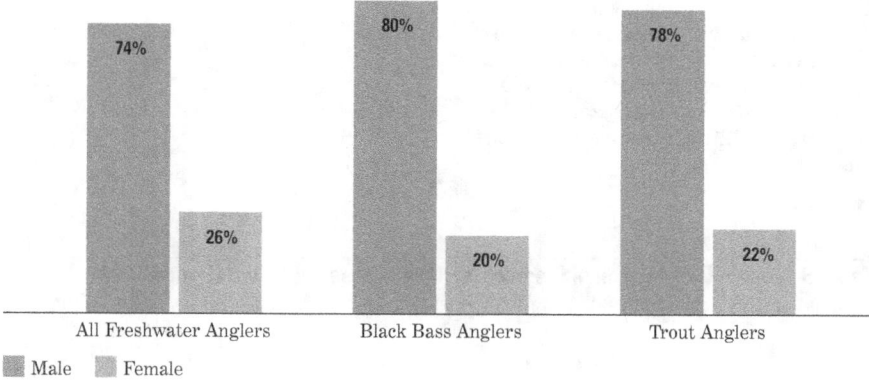

Figure 5. Education Distribution of Freshwater, Black Bass, and Trout Anglers: 2001
(Population 16 years of age and older. Excludes Great Lakes fishing.)

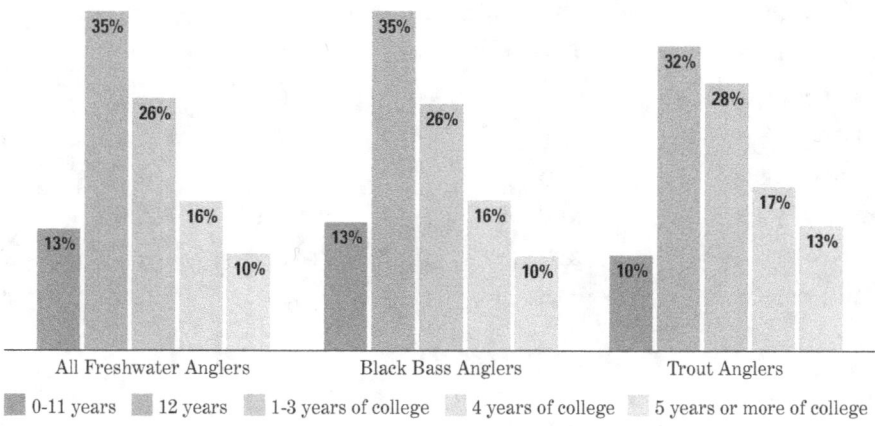

Income
Table 8 indicates that both bass and trout anglers have higher incomes than all freshwater anglers. 60% of trout anglers and 58% of bass anglers have incomes of $40,000 or more, which compares to 54% of all freshwater anglers. Trout anglers also have a smaller share of anglers with less than $25,000. 9% of trout anglers have incomes of less than $25,000 compared to 12% of freshwater and bass anglers.

Table 8. Income Distribution of Freshwater, Black Bass, and Trout Anglers: 2001
(Population 16 years of age and older. Numbers in thousands. Excludes Great Lakes fishing.)

Income	All Freshwater Anglers		Black Bass Anglers			Trout Anglers		
	Number	Percent	Number	Percent	Percent of Freshwater	Number	Percent	Percent of Freshwater
U.S. Total	27,913	100%	10,708	100%	38%	7,819	100%	28%
Not Reported	4,178	15%	1,457	14%	35%	1,075	14%	26%
Under $10,000	755	3%	245	2%	32%	156	2%	21%
$10,000–$19,999	1,413	5%	485	5%	34%	282	4%	20%
$20,000–$24,999	1,223	4%	505	5%	41%	241	3%	20%
$25,000–$29,999	1,539	6%	535	5%	35%	372	5%	24%
$30,000–$34,999	1,743	6%	634	6%	36%	533	7%	31%
$35,000–$39,999	1,640	6%	703	7%	43%	447	6%	27%
$40,000–$49,999	3,152	11%	1,283	12%	41%	842	11%	27%
$50,000–$74,999	5,920	21%	2,316	22%	39%	1,791	23%	30%
$75,000–$99,999	3,205	11%	1,239	12%	39%	1,050	13%	33%
$100,000 or More	3,146	11%	1,307	12%	42%	1,030	13%	33%

Part Three—Expenditures

This section examines spending made pursuant to freshwater fishing in 2001. It does not include spending on saltwater or Great Lakes fishing. Spending is examined by type of angler not by type of fish pursued. The different types of anglers considered include freshwater, bass, and trout, where one must participate in each respective type of fishing to be considered as such. The categories are not mutually exclusive. On the contrary, all bass anglers and trout anglers are freshwater anglers, and some bass anglers are also trout anglers and vice versa. Consequently, the spending of bass anglers includes spending made pursuant to other freshwater species such as walleye, panfish, catfish, or trout. Examining expenditures in this manner permits analysis of how the average expenditures of both bass and trout anglers differ from one another and how they both differ from all freshwater anglers.

Expenditures by type of angler and spending category are presented in Table 9. Both bass and trout anglers average higher trip expenditures than all freshwater anglers. Bass anglers spent $10.2 billion on trips and equipment made pursuant to freshwater fishing. Trout anglers spent $6.4 billion. Dividing these spending totals by the number of bass and trout anglers results in averages of $949 and $816 respectively. Bass anglers average higher spending than trout anglers and both have averages considerably higher than that of all freshwater anglers, $716.

For trip costs bass anglers average higher spending than both trout anglers and all freshwater anglers; however, there are numerous categories of trip spending in which trout anglers have higher average spending than bass anglers. Trout anglers average higher spending on food, lodging, private transportation, public transportation, guide fees, public and private land use fees, and heating fuel. The overall higher trip average for bass anglers is primarily attributable to higher spending in two categories: boating costs and bait. The average boating costs of bass anglers is nearly three times that of trout anglers.

For equipment expenditures, bass anglers average higher expenditures in nearly every category. Bass anglers average higher expenditures for rods, reels, tackle boxes, lures, depth finders, etc. However, trout anglers average higher spending for auxiliary equipment such as camping equipment and clothing, which can also be used for other types of outdoor recreation, but is primarily used for fishing.

Bass anglers average substantially higher special equipment expenditures. They average $342 compared to $240 for trout anglers and $255 for all freshwater anglers. Further inspection reveals that this is primarily due to higher spending of bass anglers on boats and recreational vehicles such as vans, motor homes, and campers.

Table 9. Expenditures of All Freshwater, Black Bass, and Trout Anglers: 2001
(Population 16 years of age and older. In thousands of dollars, except for averages. Excludes Great Lakes fishing.)

	All Freshwater	Average Freshwater	Black Bass Anglers	Average Bass	Trout Anglers	Average Trout
Total, all items	19,972,014	716	10,162,305	949	6,383,055	816
Trip-Related Expenditures						
Total trip-related	9,392,904	337	4,679,998	437	3,354,867	429
Food and lodging, total	4,028,437	144	1,908,179	178	1,534,506	196
Food	2,923,180	105	1,412,445	132	1,089,730	139
Lodging	1,105,257	40	495,734	46	444,776	57
Transportation, total	2,624,595	94	1,245,559	116	1,009,620	129
Public	209,056	7	85,974	8	109,058	14
Private	2,415,539	87	1,159,586	108	900,561	115
Other trip costs, total	2,739,872	98	1,526,260	143	810,742	104
Guide fees, pack trip or package fees	236,495	8	119,622	11	109,570	14
Public land use fees	90,904	3	46,927	4	39,228	5
Private land use fees	67,731	2	33,386	3	24,040	3
Equipment rental	128,813	5	66,252	6	58,027	7
Boating costs	1,194,849	43	737,716	69	267,076	34
Heating and cooking fuel	67,266	2	27,762	3	27,648	4
Bait	761,793	27	392,269	37	219,547	28
Ice	192,022	7	102,327	10	65,607	8
Equipment Expenses						
Fishing Equipment	2,959,515	106	1,589,669	148	931,887	119
Rods, reels, poles and rodmaking components	1,171,010	42	620,420	58	393,387	50
Lines and leaders	305,802	11	162,881	15	105,497	13
Artificial lures, flies, baits and dressing	585,275	21	349,775	33	197,248	25
Hooks, sinkers, and swivels	228,785	8	117,815	11	72,172	9
Tackle boxes	91,603	3	55,461	5	28,286	4
Creels, stringers, fish bags and landing gear	63,898	2	31,563	3	16,618	2
Minnow traps, seines, and bait containers	33,064	1	19,948	2	5,768	1
Depth and fish finders, and other electronics	228,855	8	108,756	10	31,694	4
Ice fishing equipment	77,867	3	28,811	3	17,440	2
Other fishing equipment	173,356	6	94,240	9	63,777	8
Auxillary equipment	498,449	18	234,775	22	217,414	28
Camping equipment	278,991	10	122,416	11	117,511	15
Binoculars, spotting scopes	17,875	1	10,593	1	7,032	1
Special fishing and hunting clothing, boots, foul weather gear	159,143	6	77,732	7	79,048	10
Other	27,445	1	12,313	1	10,980	1
Special equipment	7,121,146	255	3,657,862	342	1,878,887	240

Note: "Special equipment" includes purchases of big ticket items such as boats, campers, trucks, and cabins that are primarily purchased for use in wildlife-related recreation.

Note: Spending is examined here by type of angler (freshwater, bass, and trout) not by type of fish pursued. One must participate in each respective type of fishing to be considered as such. The categories are not mutually exclusive. On the contrary, all bass anglers and trout anglers are freshwater anglers, and some bass anglers are also trout anglers and vice versa. Consequently, the spending of bass anglers includes spending made pursuant to other freshwater species such as walleye, panfish, or catfish.

Part Four—Boat Usage

This section examines the socioeconomic characteristics of anglers who use boats for fishing. A respondent is identified as a boating angler or boater if he or she fished from a boat at least one day during 2001. The boating referred to herein only concerns that portion of all boating that is related to fishing, and anglers who are considered boaters are those who fish from a boat regardless of their use of boats for purposes other than fishing. Examining the socioeconomic characteristics of those anglers who boated at least one day permits an understanding of what variables are associated with higher boating participation.

Table 10 presents socioeconomic characteristics of freshwater, bass, and trout anglers who boated. The columns indicate the total number of freshwater, bass, and trout anglers, how many of each boated, and what percent were boaters. For example, the first row and first column of Table 10 indicates there were 27.9 million freshwater anglers in 2001. The second column indicates that 14.8 million freshwater anglers fished from a boat. The third column indicates that the 14.8 million boaters represent 53% of all freshwater anglers.

Overall 53% of freshwater anglers, 65% of bass anglers, and 48% of trout anglers fished from a boat at least one day. Deviations from these overall percentages in the rows indicates characteristics that are associated with higher or lower boating participation.

Fred Youngblood/USFWS

Population Size of Residence
The population size of residence is measured in terms of metropolitan statistical area (MSA). "The general concept of a metropolitan . . . statistical area is that of a core area containing a substantial population nucleus, together with adjacent communities having a high degree of economic and social integration with that core . . . Each metropolitan statistical area must have at least one urbanized area of 50,000 or more inhabitants. "

Consequently, classification by MSA provides information on the population of angler residences. The categories of MSA listed in Table 10 indicate whether an angler lived in a MSA of various sizes or lived outside a MSA, which indicates a more rural residency.

The proportion of anglers that participated in boating varies little with respect to MSA. For all freshwater anglers the percentage of boating is slightly higher among those anglers that reside in MSAs of 50,000–249,999 and 250,000–999,999, where the percentages rise to 56% and 55% respectively. For bass anglers the percentage is highest among those who reside in MSAs 250,000–999,999, and for trout anglers it is highest for those in MSAs of 50,000–249,999.

Table 10. Selected Characteristics of Freshwater, Bass, and Trout Anglers who Use Boats for Fishing
(Population 16 years of age and older. Numbers in thousands. Excludes Great Lakes fishing.)

	All Freshwater Anglers	Freshwater Boaters	Percent	Black Bass Anglers	Black Bass Boaters	Percent	Trout Anglers	Trout Boaters	Percent
Total All Persons	**27,913**	**14,787**	**53%**	**10,708**	**6,993**	**65%**	**7,819**	**3,720**	**48%**
Population Size of Residence									
Metropolitan statistical area (MSA)	19,136	10,217	53%	7,618	5,029	66%	5,704	2,788	49%
1,000,000 or more	10,220	5,292	52%	3,966	2,529	64%	3,601	1,733	48%
250,000 to 999,999	5,638	3,088	55%	2,533	1,747	69%	1,304	637	49%
50,000 to 249,999	3,278	1,838	56%	1,119	753	67%	798	418	52%
Outside MSA	8,777	4,569	52%	3,090	1,963	64%	2,115	932	44%
Census Geographic Region									
New England	1,030	539	52%	463	297	64%	566	295	52%
Middle Atlantic	2,113	911	43%	990	619	63%	1,017	347	34%
East North Central	4,790	2,727	57%	1,956	1,326	68%	517	329	64%
West North Central	3,749	2,235	60%	1,221	765	63%	364	160	44%
South Atlantic	4,629	2,382	51%	2,164	1,397	65%	729	356	49%
East South Central	2,356	1,313	56%	1,171	773	66%	214	105	49%
West South Central	3,661	1,954	53%	1,661	1,087	65%	500	255	51%
Mountain	2,393	1,012	42%	427	259	61%	1,873	749	40%
Pacific	3,198	1,715	54%	655	471	72%	2,040	1,124	55%
Age									
16–17	1,146	557	49%	500	315	63%	350	164	47%
18–24	2,576	1,227	48%	1,056	637	60%	663	264	40%
25–34	5,452	2,782	51%	2,200	1,415	64%	1,540	695	45%
35–44	7,492	3,847	51%	2,979	1,851	62%	2,261	1,130	50%
45–54	5,469	3,121	57%	2,005	1,417	71%	1,564	765	49%
55–64	3,310	1,988	60%	1,171	866	74%	798	420	53%
65+	2,469	1,265	51%	797	491	62%	643	283	44%
Gender									
Male	20,729	11,502	55%	8,615	5,716	66%	6,110	3,007	49%
Female	7,184	3,285	46%	2,093	1,277	61%	1,709	713	42%
Ethnicity									
Hispanic	1,081	382	35%	349	185	53%	426	166	39%
Non-Hispanic	26,832	14,405	54%	10,359	6,807	66%	7,393	3,554	48%
Race									
White	26,176	14,143	54%	10,122	6,697	66%	7,489	3,578	48%
Black	1,235	470	38%	436	238	55%	124	56	45%
Asian	198	43	22%	77	**	**	57	**	**
All Others	304	130	43%	*73	*42	*57%	*126	*40	*32%

continues

Table 10. Selected Characteristics of Freshwater, Bass, and Trout Anglers who Use Boats for Fishing – continued
(Population 16 years of age and older. Numbers in thousands. Excludes Great Lakes fishing.)

	All Freshwater Anglers	Freshwater Boaters	Percent	Black Bass Anglers	Black Bass Boaters	Percent	Trout Anglers	Trout Boaters	Percent
Annual Household Income									
Under $10,000	755	299	40%	245	121	49%	156	64	41%
$10,000–$19,999	1,413	666	47%	485	278	57%	282	147	52%
$20,000–$24,999	1,223	637	52%	505	351	70%	241	112	46%
$25,000–$29,999	1,539	692	45%	535	340	64%	372	167	45%
$30,000–$34,999	1,743	838	48%	634	389	61%	533	220	41%
$35,000–$39,999	1,640	862	53%	703	413	59%	447	228	51%
$40,000–$49,999	3,152	1,786	57%	1,283	842	66%	842	437	52%
$50,000–$74,999	5,920	3,248	55%	2,316	1,532	66%	1,791	844	47%
$75,000–$99,999	3,205	1,790	56%	1,239	847	68%	1,050	490	47%
$100,000 or More	3,146	1,841	59%	1,307	920	70%	1,030	521	51%
Not Reported	4,178	2,128	51%	1,457	959	66%	1,075	490	46%
Education									
11 years or less	3,539	1,651	47%	1,434	869	61%	777	347	45%
12 years	9,842	5,150	52%	3,781	2,480	66%	2,489	1,167	47%
1–3 years of college	7,362	4,136	56%	2,765	1,819	66%	2,191	1,066	49%
4 years of college	4,346	2,382	55%	1,679	1,170	70%	1,339	639	48%
5 years or more of college	2,824	1,468	52%	1,049	654	62%	1,023	501	49%

*Estimate based on small sample size.
**Sample size too small to report data reliably.

Census Geographic Region

Boating participation differs considerably by geographic region of residence. However, the percent of bass anglers who use boats is relatively consistent compared to all freshwater and trout anglers. For all freshwater anglers the percentage of boaters ranges from a high of 60% in the West North Central to a low of 42% in the Mountain region. For trout anglers the percentage ranges from 64% in the East North Central to 34% in the Middle Atlantic. For bass anglers, most regions have percentages that are relatively close to the overall average of 65%. The Pacific has the highest percentage at 72%, and Mountain has the lowest at 61%. Figure 6 presents a graphical display of the percent of all freshwater, trout, and bass anglers who participate in boating by region.

State of Residence

Table 11 presents geographic differences in boating at the state level. Besides presenting geographic differences at a more refined level than regional, which appears in Table 10, the information presented here is by state where fishing occurred rather than by place of residence. Given the differences in fishable water that occurs among states, it is not surprising to find that the percent of boating participation differs considerably. Also unsurprising is that the "Land of 10,000 Lakes," Minnesota, has the highest percentage of freshwater anglers who use boats at 84%. Other prominent lake fishing states in the Midwest such as Wisconsin and Michigan closely follow at 79% and 71% respectively. States with a high proportion of river fishing such as New Mexico, West Virginia, or Colorado have comparatively lower share of freshwater boating anglers, at 26%, 34%, and 39% respectively.

Age

The percentage of anglers who use boats is positively correlated with age. In other words, as age increases so too does the percentage of anglers that use boats. Anglers 18–24 years old have the lowest percentage of boaters. This is the case for all freshwater, bass, and trout anglers. The highest percentage of boaters is also the same among the different types of anglers: 55–64 years old. As well, beyond 64 the percentage of boaters declines for each.

Gender

Male freshwater, bass, and trout anglers are more likely to be boaters than females. 55% of male freshwater anglers use boats compared to 46% of female. Similarly, 66% of male bass anglers and 49% of male trout anglers use boats compared to 61% and 42% of females.

Figure 6. Percent of All Freshwater, Trout, and Bass Anglers Who Use Boats for Fishing in the Bureau of Census Regions

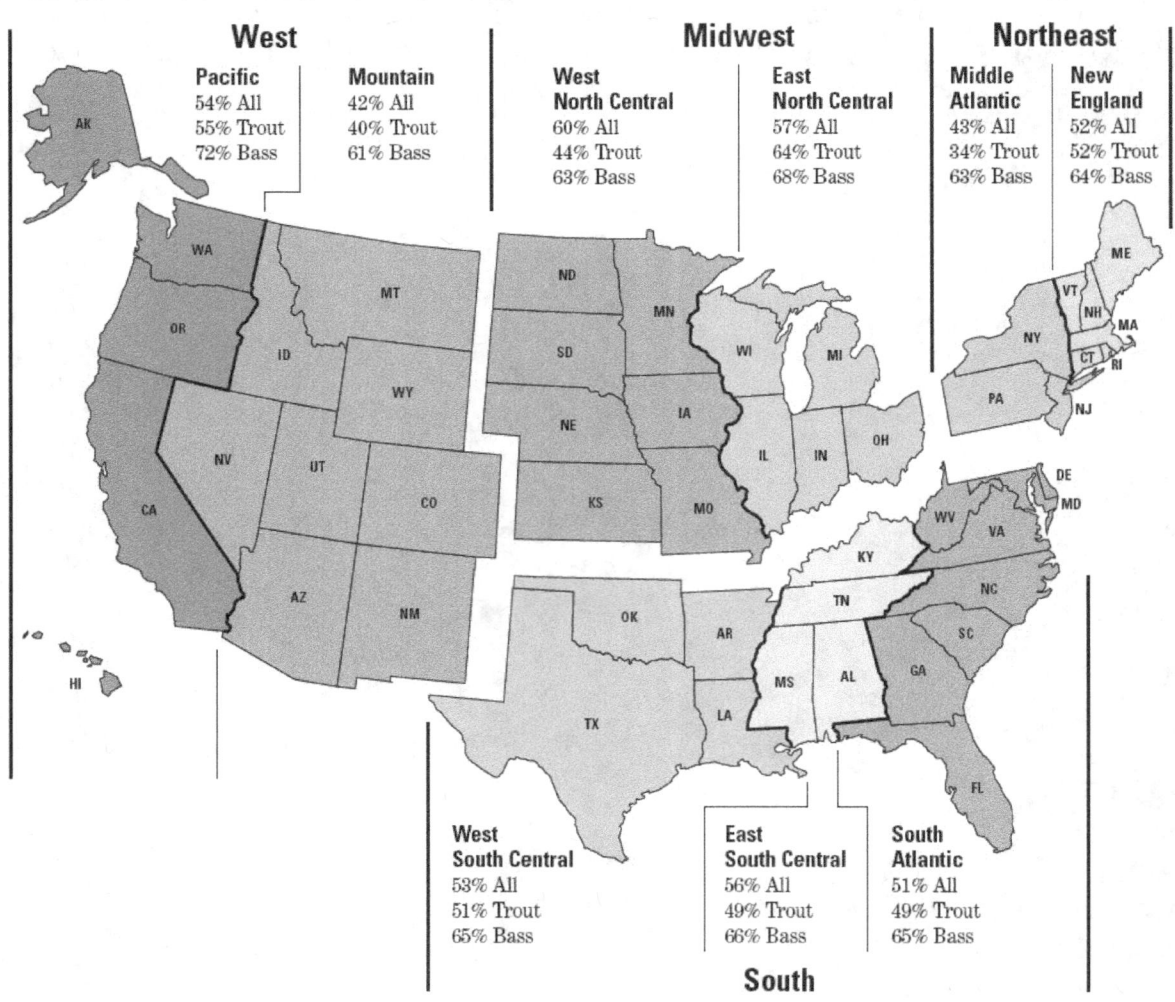

Ethnicity

Hispanic anglers are less likely to be boaters. For each type of angler, the percent of Hispanics that boat is notably lower than Non-Hispanics.

Race

White anglers are more likely than other races to use boats. 54% of Whites who fish in freshwater are boaters, which compares to 38% of Blacks, 22% of Asians, and 43% of other races. 66% of White bass anglers are boaters compared to 55% of Blacks and 57% of other races. Likewise, 48% of White trout anglers are boaters compared to 45% of Blacks and 32% of others.

Annual Household Income

Higher incomes are generally associated with a higher percentage of boaters. The percentage of anglers who are boaters does not rise consistently as incomes increase, but generally shows a positive correlation. For every type of angler, those who are the least likely to be boaters are those with the lowest incomes. For freshwater anglers, those with incomes of $100,000 or more have the highest percentage of boaters. For bass anglers the highest proportion of boaters are those with incomes of $100,000 or more and those with incomes of $20,000–$24,999. For trout anglers, a positive correlation between income and boating participation is less discernable.

Education

There is some variation in boating participation rates with respect to level of education. The lowest percentage of boaters for every type of angler is among those with less than 12 years of education. For freshwater anglers, those with the highest percent of boating have 1–3 years of college. For bass anglers those with 4 years of college have the highest percentage, and for trout anglers those with 1–3 years of college and 5 or more years of college share the peak.

Table 11. Boating Participation by State where Fishing Occurred

(Population 16 years of age and older. Numbers in thousands.)

	All Freshwater Anglers	Freshwater Boaters	Freshwater Percent	Black Bass Anglers Percent Boaters	Trout Anglers Percent Boaters
U.S. Total	27,913	14,787	53%	65%	48%
AK	266	159	60%	**	57%
AL	732	470	64%	72%	*92%
AR	782	533	68%	81%	*57%
AZ	419	211	50%	60%	45%
CA	1,865	964	52%	70%	52%
CO	915	361	40%	*39%	39%
CT	255	125	49%	68%	43%
DE	73	38	52%	63%	*39%
FL	1,316	759	58%	72%	**
GA	1,017	522	51%	67%	*55%
HI	*12	**	**	**	**
IA	542	268	50%	54%	**
ID	416	198	48%	*63%	44%
IL	1,060	479	45%	55%	**
IN	746	385	52%	63%	**
KS	404	184	46%	61%	**
KY	780	425	55%	62%	**
LA	659	450	68%	83%	**
MA	325	157	48%	60%	39%
MD	367	197	54%	68%	*42%
ME	272	189	69%	74%	68%
MI	980	697	71%	88%	76%
MN	1,560	1,313	84%	89%	*70%
MO	1,215	587	48%	59%	42%
MS	494	280	57%	65%	**
MT	349	159	46%	*61%	45%
NC	848	470	56%	64%	*57%
ND	179	120	67%	**	**
NE	296	160	54%	55%	*61%
NH	221	132	60%	72%	61%
NJ	331	164	50%	59%	56%
NM	314	80	26%	*51%	21%
NV	172	85	50%	*68%	47%
NY	901	459	51%	72%	42%
OH	1,081	494	46%	57%	*61%
OK	774	367	47%	62%	**
OR	611	383	63%	*70%	59%
PA	1,163	469	40%	60%	29%
RI	51	27	53%	*61%	*51%
SC	591	387	66%	77%	*59%
SD	214	133	62%	*81%	**
TN	903	552	61%	76%	*45%
TX	1,842	947	51%	59%	**
UT	517	265	51%	86%	51%
VA	721	411	57%	62%	*35%
VT	171	90	52%	74%	50%
WA	659	398	60%	80%	62%
WI	1,307	1,032	79%	89%	*77%
WV	318	107	34%	49%	43%
WY	293	134	46%	**	44%

*Estimate based on small sample size.
**Sample size too small to report data reliably.

Part Five—Fishing by Boat Model

The descriptive statistics contained in Table 10 and the adjoining discussion address variations in the rate of boating participation by angler characteristics. As noted, numerous variables appear to have some relationship with boating participation. This section summarizes the results of a regression analysis on participation in *some boating* and *avid boating*. *Some boating* is defined as at least one day of boat use while fishing. *Avid boating* is defined as greater than 16 days of boating while fishing. Only 25% of freshwater anglers used boats for fishing more than 16 days in 2001. Thus, anglers in the top 25% of boating days are considered avid boaters. Regression analysis can be used to evaluate whether different variables have a significant impact on angler participation in *some boating* and *avid boating*.

The use of descriptive statistics alone as in Table 10 is not the appropriate method to test the validity of a relationship between the various characteristics and boating participation. There are interrelationships among the characteristic variables themselves that can act to conceal the effect of each on participation. For example, the participation rate increases as income increases and as age increases. However, income also tends to increase with age. This cross correlation acts to conceal the independent impact that age and income have on participation. By using regression, the effect of each on the probability of boating participation can be isolated more effectively. Additionally, regression permits assessment of whether the correlations of the different variables with boating participation are significant. In other words it permits an assessment of the probability that the relationship occurred by chance.

The model employed is a continuation ratio logit regression model. Essentially this model treats boating participation as a progression of stages: from *no boating* to *some boating*, and then *some boating* to *avid boating*. Graphically this progression of stages is represented in Figure 7.

Figure 7.

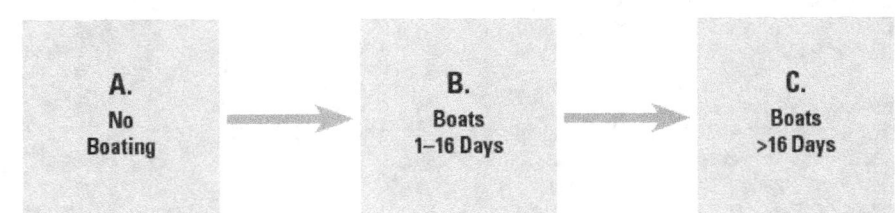

This model permits an assessment of the impact that numerous variables have on the probability of participation in *some boating*. Additionally, the model permits an assessment of how the same variables impact the probability that anglers will participate in *avid boating* given that they participate in *some boating*. By using the continuation ratio model, one can assess what variables are relatively important in determining if an angler will participate in *some boating* and what variables are relatively important for assessing whether an angler will participate in *avid boating*.

In this analysis there are separate regressions for bass and trout anglers. The majority of factors important in affecting the probability that a bass angler will participate in *some boating* and *avid boating* have a similar effect for trout anglers, but there are some differences. A summary of the results is presented here and more detailed explanations of the model, variables, and results are in Appendix A.

For both trout and bass anglers, increasing an angler's income has a significant positive impact on his or her likelihood of participation in *some boating*, but not *avid boating*. If anything, the results suggest that likelihood of participation in *avid boating* may actually go down as income increases. This could result because those with higher incomes spend fewer days participating in leisure activities, or perhaps they do engage in similar levels

of leisure, but their activities are more diverse. However, the lack of statistical significance does not encourage full confidence in the negative results.

Among bass anglers, age does not have a significant impact on participation in *some boating*. That is, all other things equal, older anglers are not significantly more likely to participate in *some boating* than younger anglers. However, it does have a significant positive impact on participation in *avid boating*. For bass anglers, the probability of *avid boating* increases with age. These results could suggest that greater leisure time associated with retirement is particularly important in determining whether a bass angler will be an avid boater.

The results for boating participation by age for trout anglers differ from those of bass anglers. Older bass anglers are significantly more likely to participate in *avid boating*, but for trout anglers this is not the case. However, older trout anglers are significantly more likely to participate in *some boating*.

Anglers residing in different states have relatively greater variation in likelihood of participation in *some boating* than *avid boating*. It is not surprising that residents of some states are more likely to participate in boating than others. Some states may possess weather that is more suitable for boating than others, and some may possess a relatively plentiful supply of boatable water. Consequently, it is not surprising that anglers who reside in some states are more likely to participate in boating than others. Among both trout and bass anglers, significant differences in likelihood of *some boating* between states are common. However, residents of relatively few states exhibit significant differences in likelihood of *avid boating*. Whatever the cause of differences in *some boating* among states, water accessibility, climate, etc., their impacts on participation in *avid boating* are less pronounced.

Table 12 presents the states whose residents are most likely to use boats while fishing. These states come from the clusters with the highest coefficients in the regressions. The table is segmented by bass and trout anglers. Fishing for each respective species need not occur in the state of residence. Consequently, those who sought bass and resided in Hawaii did not necessarily fish for bass there. They likely fished for bass while visiting other states.

Among both trout and bass anglers, the likelihood of females participating in *some boating* is not significantly different than males. However, females are significantly less likely than males to participate in *avid boating*.

Among bass anglers, Blacks and Other Races are significantly less likely to participate in *some boating* than Whites. However, given that they participate in *some boating*, there is no significant difference in likelihood of *avid boating* among Blacks, Other Races, and Whites. Among trout anglers, there is no significant difference among the races for participation in either *some boating* or *avid boating*.

The results largely suggest that anglers residing in metropolitan statistical areas (MSAs) of various sizes are no less likely to participate in *some boating* than those residing outside MSAs. This is the case for both bass and trout anglers. For bass anglers, those residing in mid-sized MSAs of 250,000–999,999 are actually significantly more likely to participate in some boating than those who reside outside MSAs. Otherwise, residents of MSAs of various sizes have no statistically significant difference in likelihood of *some boating*. Even bass and trout anglers who reside in the largest metropolitan areas, MSAs of one million residents or more, do not have significantly different participation in boating than those who reside outside MSAs.

Residents of large metropolitan areas have a lower participation rate in fishing than residents of non-metropolitan areas. For U.S. residents over 16 years old, 21% of those who live outside MSAs freshwater fish compared to 9% of those who live in MSAs of 1,000,000 or more. However, given that individuals do participate in freshwater fishing, the likelihood of fishing from a boat is not significantly different whether they reside in or outside a MSA.

For bass anglers the results also indicate that differences in the likelihood of participation in *avid boating* between residents of large metropolitan areas and non-metropolitan areas are not significant; however, for trout anglers this is not the case. Trout anglers who reside in small to mid-sized metropolitan areas are more likely to participate in *avid boating* than those who reside outside metropolitan areas.

Both bass and trout anglers who purchase books and magazines related to fishing are significantly more likely to participate in both *some boating* and *avid boating*. For businesses interested in marketing products to anglers who are boaters, these results suggest that print media may be effective in reaching this audience. However, print media will likely be less effective in reaching anglers who are not boaters because anglers who purchase books and magazines are less likely to be non-boaters.

There are several different species of fish that, if pursued, are associated with a significantly higher rate of participation in *some boating* or *avid boating*. Interestingly several of the same species variables are associated with higher boating participation among both trout and bass anglers: crappie, striped bass, walleye, pike, and freshwater salmon. Conversely, bass anglers who also pursue catfish or steelhead have a lower probability of participating in *some boating*.

Trout anglers who seek numerous different other fish species are significantly more likely to participate in *some boating*, but for bass anglers this is not the case. If anything, the data suggest that bass anglers who are more specialized in the fish that they seek are more likely to participate in boating.

Table 12. States whose Residents are Most Likely to Participate in Some Boating while Fishing

Bass Anglers	Trout Anglers
AR	AL
FL	AR
HI	FL
LA	LA
ME	ME
MI	MI
MN	MS
ND	NE
NH	NH
SC	SC
SD	WA
UT	WI
WA	
WI	
WY	

Some Boating refers to boating 1 to 16 days while fishing.

Several variables related to the hunting activities of anglers are associated with significant differences in boating participation. Bass anglers who hunt deer or small game are significantly more likely to participate in *some boating*. Deer hunters are also significantly more likely to participate in *avid boating*. These results may be useful from a marketing perspective. If a manufacturer is interested in marketing a product to all boaters or avid boaters, these results suggest that knowledge of participation in deer hunting could be useful. Trout anglers who hunt for numerous different species of game are significantly more likely to participate in *some boating* and *avid boating*. A possible explanation for this result is that those who hunt numerous species are likely to be more avid outdoor recreationists.

Summary

In 2001, there were 10.7 million black bass and 7.8 million trout anglers in the U.S, who pursued bass nearly 160 million days and trout 83 million days. Participation rates for both bass and trout fishing vary dramatically among the different states. The wide variations are attributable to differences in freshwater habitat, which often favor one species over the other. Consequently, it is not unusual to find that states with high participation rates for bass fishing have low participation in trout fishing and vice versa.

Expenditures by bass and trout anglers reveal the economic importance of both recreational fish species. In 2001 bass anglers spent $10.2 billion on trips and equipment made pursuant to freshwater fishing, and trout anglers spent $6.4 billion. Bass anglers averaged higher equipment and trip-related spending than trout anglers, but average spending by both bass and trout anglers was greater than that of all freshwater anglers.

From a socioeconomic perspective, all freshwater, bass, and trout anglers have similarities and differences. They have a similar distribution of participants by age of the angler, with individuals who are 35–44 years old comprising the majority of participants for each. Females comprise a higher proportion of all freshwater anglers than they do of either bass or trout anglers. Females are more heavily concentrated among anglers who seek species such as panfish, catfish, or any freshwater fish. Bass anglers and all freshwater anglers have a similar educational distribution, but trout anglers have a slightly higher proportion with four years of college or more. Both bass and trout anglers have higher incomes on average than do all freshwater anglers.

Fishing by boat is an important method of fishing for both bass and trout anglers. There are numerous socioeconomic characteristics associated with different rates of boating participation. Overall, 65% of bass anglers and 48% of trout anglers fished from a boat at least one day in 2001.

Regression analysis reveals that several characteristics have a significant positive or negative impact on either participation in *some boating* or *avid boating*, where *some boating* is defined as fishing from a boat 1–16 days, and *avid boating* is defined as fishing from a boat for more than 16 days. For both trout and bass anglers there are several characteristics that have a significant positive impact on either *some boating* or *avid boating*: rising income, purchasing fishing related books or magazines, and increasing age. Bass and trout anglers who also seek other fish species such as crappie, striped bass, walleye, pike, and freshwater salmon are significantly more likely to participate in *some boating*. Conversely, bass anglers who also pursue catfish or steelhead have a lower probability of participating in *some boating*.

Regression analysis also reveals that there are several variables concerning the hunting activities of anglers that are associated with significant differences in boating participation. Bass anglers who hunt small game are significantly more likely to participate in *some boating*, and bass anglers who hunt deer are significantly more likely to participate in both *some boating* and *avid boating*. Trout anglers who hunt numerous species of animals are more likely to participate in both *some boating* and *avid boating*.

Fishing remains one of the most prominent recreational activities in the U.S. It truly is a long standing tradition that continues to retain appeal despite the emergence of numerous other outlets for leisure time. Fishing is not only important as a leisure activity, it is also a powerful engine of economic growth. In 2001 anglers spent a total of $28.4 billion on freshwater and Great Lakes fishing. This $28.4 billion generated an estimated $74.8 billion in economic output, $4.8 billion in tax revenue, and 683,892 jobs.[5] Bass and trout are two of the most pursued freshwater species by anglers. Consequently, they are of vital importance as a leisure resource and catalyst for economic growth.

---

[5] *Sportfishing in America*, American Sportfishing Association 2002.

Appendix A

The Model

As discussed in Part Five, the continuation ratio model is used in situations where ordered categories of the dependent variable represent a progression of stages, so individuals must pass through each lower stage before they go on to higher stages.

The data are partitioned into three groups, A, B, and C, as shown in Figure 7 on page 22. Logit regression is then used to estimate the logarithm of the odds ratio that an angler was in group B rather than group A. A second regression estimates the logarithm of the odds ratio that an angler was in group C rather than group B. The analysis was performed for bass and trout anglers separately, so there are two sets of results. With two regressions apiece, the total number of regressions is four.

Variables

The explanatory variables used in the models are contained in Table A-1. The bass and trout models have many of the same variables, but there are some differences.

The variables used in the regression were selected from a large set of potential explanatory variables through a combination of Stepwise Model Fitting and use of the likelihood ratio test.[6] Many of the variables are nominal variables. Each nominal variable used in the regressions has a base or reference case. The reference case is given a value of zero in the estimated equation. Consequently, the calculated coefficient for the reference case is embodied in the

coefficient for the intercept term. The reference case for each nominal variable is given by the first level for each in Table A-1. Thus, the reference case for the bass angler regressions is as follows:

- Residents of state cluster number one

- Male

- Lives outside a MSA

- Did not hunt deer or small game

- Did not fish for crappie, striped bass, catfish, walleye, pike, freshwater salmon, steelhead, saltwater salmon, or redfish

- Has five years of college or more

Every variable value other than the reference case has a coefficient. For each regression these coefficients indicate the change in the log odds that occurs when the value of the respective nominal variable is different than the reference case. For example, since "Five years of college or more" is the reference case for EDUC, each of the other levels ("Less than four years of college," and "Four years of college") will have a coefficient. The coefficient for "Four years of college" will indicate the change in the log odds that results because a bass angler had four years of college rather than five years of college or more.

The CL_BASS and CL_TROUT variables are clusters of states. The states are partitioned into clusters such that states in the same cluster are more similar to each other in terms of boating participation rate than with states in different clusters. Why states within a cluster are similar in terms of boating participation is not known: it could be that anglers within the states have similar access to boatable water, or it could be that states share similar climate, which could make boating more or less appealing. What is known is that the states within a cluster are more similar with regard to boating participation than they are with states in other clusters. The clusters for bass anglers and trout anglers were both created using the Greenacre procedure, which utilizes a form of chi-square distancing.

The FISHCOUNT and HUNTCOUNT variables in the trout angler regressions indicate how many total different species were pursued through fishing and hunting. FISHCOUNT indicates the total number of different species that were pursued while fishing in 2001, and HUNTCOUNT indicates the total number of different species that were pursued while hunting in 2001.

---

[6] Consult author for additional information on other model specifications, list of variables that were not included in the final regression, and information on Stepwise Model Fitting.

Table A-1. Regression Explanatory Variables

Bass Anglers		Trout Anglers	
INCOME	Ordinal variable with 10 levels, treated as continuous*	INCOME	Ordinal variable with 10 levels, treated as continuous*
AGE	Age of recreationist in years for those older than 15	AGE	Age of recreationist in years for those older than 15
CL_BASS	Nominal variable with 6 levels that represent clusters of states One = CT, ID, IN, MA, MD, MS, MT, NC, NJ, NV, OK, RI, TX, VA Two = AZ, CO, DE, IA, KS, KY, MO, NE, NM, OH, PA Three = AR, FL, ME, NH, SC, UT Four = AL, CA, GA, IL, NY, OR, TN, VT Five = HI, LA, MI, MN, ND, SD, WA, WI, WY Six = WV	CL_TROUT	Nominal variable with 6 levels that represent clusters of states One = AK, CA, CT, DE, NC, NJ, OH, OK, RI, UT Two = AZ, HI, ID, KS, MA, MD, MT, NV, NY, SD, TN, TX, WV, WY Three = GA, IL, IN, MN, ND, OR, VT Four = CO, IA, KY, MO, NM, PA, VA Five = FL, ME, MS, NE, NH, SC, WA Six = AL, AR, LA, MI, WI
SEX	Indicator variable with 2 values to indicate respondent gender Male Female	SEX	Indicator variable with 2 values to indicate respondent gender Male Female
FISHBOOK	Indicator variable with 2 values Did not purchase books or magazines pertaining to fishing Purchased books or magazines pertaining to fishing	FISHBOOK	Indicator variable with 2 values Did not purchase books or magazines pertaining to fishing Purchased books or magazines pertaining to fishing
MSA	Nominal variable with 4 levels to indicate size of residence 1, 000, 000 or more 250, 000–999, 999 50, 000–249, 999 Outside MSA	MSA	Nominal variable with 4 levels to indicate size of residence 1, 000, 000 or more 250, 000–999, 999 50, 000–249, 999 Outside MSA
RACE	Nominal variable with 3 levels to indicate race White Asian Black Other Races	TURKEY	Indicator variable with 2 values Did Not Hunt Turkey Hunted Turkey
SMALLGAME	Indicator variable with 2 values Did Not Hunt Small Game Hunted Small Game	CRAPPIE	Indicator variable with 2 values Did Not fish for crappie Fished for crappie
DEER	Indicator variable with 2 values Did Not Hunt Deer Hunted Deer	STRIPED	Indicator variable with 2 values Did Not fish for striped bass Fished for striped bass
CRAPPIE	Indicator variable with 2 values Did Not fish for crappie Fished for crappie	WALLEYE	Indicator variable with 2 values Did Not fish for walleye Fished for walleye
STRIPED	Indicator variable with 2 values Did Not fish for striped bass Fished for striped bass	PIKE	Indicator variable with 2 values Did Not fish for pike Fished for pike

Table A-1. Regression Explanatory Variables

Bass Anglers		Trout Anglers	
WALLEYE	Indicator variable with 2 values Did Not fish for walleye Fished for walleye	SALMON_F	Indicator variable with 2 values Did Not fish for salmon in freswater Fished for salmon in freswater
PIKE	Indicator variable with 2 values Did Not fish for pike Fished for pike	OTHER	Indicator variable with 2 values Did Not fish for other freshwater species Fished for other freshwater species
SALMON_F	Indicator variable with 2 values Did Not fish for salmon in freswater	FISHCOUNT	Number of species other than trout that were pursued
STEELHEAD	Indicator variable with 2 values Did Not fish for steelhead Fished for steelhead	HUNTCOUNT	Number of species other than trout that were pursued
SALMON_S	Indicator variable with 2 values Did Not fish for salmon in saltwater Fished for salmon in saltwater		
REDFISH	Indicator variable with 2 values Did Not fish for redfish Fished for redfish		
EDUC	Nominal variable with 5 levels to indicate years of education 5 years or more of college 4 years of college Less than 4 years of college		

The levels of INCOME are as follows: Under $10,000, $10,000–$19,999, $20,000–$24,999, $25,000–$29,999, $30,000–$34,999, $35,000–$39,999, $40,000–$49,999, $50,000–$74,999, $75,000–$99,999, $100,000 or More.

Results

Bass Anglers

The regression results for "*No boating to Some boating*" and "*Some boating to Avid boating*" are displayed separately in Table A-2. A positive number in the "Estimate" column for "*No boating to Some boating*" indicates that the variable in question has a positive relationship with the likelihood that one participated in *some boating*. A positive number in the "Estimate" column for "*Some boating to Avid boating*" indicates that the variable in question has a positive relationship with the likelihood that one participated in *avid boating* given that he or she boated at least one day. Additionally, the Pr > ChiSq column indicates the probability that the relationship between each variable and the target variable (*some boating* or *avid boating*) occurs by chance. A Pr > ChiSq of less than 0.05 is considered strongly statistically significant, while a value of less than 0.1 is considered significant.

An example will serve to explain the particulars of Table A-2. The results for the *no boating* to *some boating* regression indicates an estimate for "Black" of –0.676. Since the base case for RACE is "White," the negative result indicates that, all other things equal, Black anglers are less likely to participate in *some boating*. Additionally, the Pr > ChiSq indicates a probability of <.0001, which is strongly significant. This significance indicates that there is greater than a 99.99% probability that the relationship between "Black" and *some boating* did not occur by chance.

All other things equal, income has a significant positive impact on probability that a bass angler will participate in *some boating*, but it does not have a significant impact on participation in *avid boating*. The estimated coefficient in the *avid boating* regression is actually negative, but it is not significant. The lack of significance indicates a relatively high probability that the relationship could have occurred by chance.

Age does not have a significant impact on participation in *some boating*. However, it does have a significant positive impact on participation in *avid boating*. As age increases the probability of *avid boating* also increases.

The results for CL_BASS indicate that geography has a significant impact on participation in *some boating*, but less so for *avid boating*. The significant differences in participation in *some boating* are numerous. However, for participation in *avid boating*, only those states in cluster three are significantly different than those in the base cluster.

Female anglers are not significantly less likely than males to participate in *some boating*. However, they are significantly less likely to participate in *avid boating*.

The results for MSA residency suggest that only those anglers that reside in mid-sized metropolitan areas of 250,000–999,999 are significantly more likely to participate in *some boating*. However, for *avid boating*, no metropolitan area is significantly different than the base case of "Outside MSA."

Blacks and Other Races are significantly less likely to participate in *some boating* than Whites. However, no race is significantly different from Whites in participation in *avid boating*.

If bass anglers purchase books and magazines pertaining to fishing, they are significantly more likely to participate in both *some boating* and *avid boating*. Moreover, the impact on the probability of *some boating* and *avid boating* is similar, as evidenced by the similar coefficients, 0.711 and 0.813.

If bass anglers also hunt for small game or deer, they are significantly more likely to participate in *some boating*. Additionally, those who hunted for deer are significantly more likely to participate in *avid boating*. These results suggest that there is a relatively good chance that deer hunters that are also bass anglers are not only boaters, but they are also avid boaters.

There are numerous other fish species that if pursued in addition to bass suggest a higher probability of both *some boating* and *avid boating*: crappie, striped bass, walleye, and pike. One possible explanation for their significance is that these species are often pursued in lakes as opposed to rivers, and lake anglers tend to use boats at a higher rate than river anglers.

Several other species suggest a higher probability of *some boating* but not *avid boating*: freshwater salmon, saltwater salmon, and redfish. Bass anglers who also pursue these species are significantly more likely to participate in *some boating* but not *avid boating*.

Anglers who also pursue catfish or steelhead have a lower probability of participating in *some boating*, but for *avid boating* the results are not significant. In other words they are neither significantly more or less likely to participate in *avid boating*.

There are some significant differences in boating participation that result from changes in education. Anglers with four years of college are significantly more likely than those with five or more years of college to participate in *some boating*. Those with less than four years of college are more likely to participate in boating than those with five or more years of college, but this result is not significant. However, for *avid boating* those with less than four years of college are significantly more likely to participate.

Table A-2. Analysis of Maximum Likelihood Estimates for Bass Anglers

Parameter	Value	No Boating to Some Boating			Some Boating to Avid Boating		
		Estimate	Chi-Square	Pr > ChiSq	Estimate	Chi-Square	Pr > ChiSq
Intercept		−0.639	6.637	0.010	−2.235	42.806	<.0001
INCOME		0.057	12.154	0.001	−0.024	1.227	0.268
AGE		0.003	0.834	0.361	0.007	3.810	0.051
CL_BASS	Two	−0.352	11.322	0.001	−0.221	2.120	0.145
CL_BASS	Three	0.530	15.430	<.0001	0.321	4.023	0.045
CL_BASS	Four	0.216	3.296	0.069	0.120	0.610	0.435
CL_BASS	Five	0.920	24.385	<.0001	0.258	1.939	0.164
CL_BASS	Six	−0.796	8.724	0.003	−0.095	0.042	0.837
SEX	Female	−0.118	1.325	0.250	−0.408	7.223	0.007
MSA	1,000,000 or more	0.022	0.044	0.834	0.014	0.001	0.921
MSA	250,000–999,999	0.273	6.184	0.013	−0.125	0.800	0.371
MSA	50,000–249,999	0.076	0.280	0.597	0.070	0.159	0.690
RACE	Asian	−0.717	1.940	0.164	0.041	0.002	0.962
RACE	Black	−0.676	10.942	0.001	−0.342	1.146	0.284
RACE	Other Races	−0.775	3.702	0.054	−0.455	0.553	0.457
FISHBOOK	Purchased	0.711	31.276	<.0001	0.813	39.942	<.0001
SMALLGAME	Hunted	0.486	16.051	<.0001	0.145	1.127	0.289
DEER	Hunted	0.315	9.076	0.003	0.360	8.200	0.004
CRAPPIE	Fished	0.400	18.384	<.0001	0.570	26.207	<.0001
STRIPED	Fished	0.441	17.414	<.0001	0.531	19.352	<.0001
CATFISH	Fished	−0.215	5.663	0.017	−0.072	0.358	0.550
WALLEYE	Fished	0.628	14.898	0.000	0.331	4.394	0.036
PIKE	Fished	0.338	4.154	0.042	0.607	13.746	0.000
SALMON_F	Fished	0.793	6.541	0.011	0.156	0.292	0.589
STEELHEAD	Fished	−0.681	2.931	0.087	−0.125	0.085	0.770
SALMON_S	Fished	1.388	3.415	0.065	−0.290	0.362	0.547
REDFISH	Fished	0.685	6.141	0.013	−0.383	1.927	0.165
EDUC	Less than four years of college	0.190	1.693	0.193	0.642	9.779	0.002
EDUC	Four years of college	0.301	3.233	0.072	0.135	0.336	0.562

Trout Anglers

As with bass anglers, trout anglers with higher incomes are also significantly more likely to participate in *some boating*. Additionally, the coefficient for income is negative in the *avid boating* regression, but, once again, the result is not significant.

Unlike bass anglers, older trout anglers are significantly more likely to participate in *some boating*. However, they are not significantly more likely to participate in *avid boating*. If anything, the negative coefficient suggests that older trout anglers are less likely to be avid boaters.

The results for the geography variable, CL_TROUT, are similar to those of bass anglers. Participation in *some boating* varies significantly by geographic region. All regions but cluster three have significantly different participation rates in *some boating*. Residents of clusters five and six are more likely to participate in boating than those in cluster one. Alternatively, residents in clusters two and four are less likely to participate. However, for *avid boating*, only residents of cluster four are significantly different than residents of cluster one. Residents of cluster four are less likely to be avid boaters.

As with bass anglers, female anglers are not significantly less likely than males to participate in *some boating*, but they are significantly less likely to participate in *avid boating*.

Trout anglers residing in metropolitan areas of all sizes are not significantly more or less likely to participate in *some boating* than anglers residing outside MSAs. However, anglers who reside in metropolitan areas of 50,000–999,999 people are significantly less likely to be avid boaters than that those who live outside MSAs.

Blacks and Other Races are significantly less likely to participate in *some boating* than Whites. However, no race is significantly different from Whites when it comes to participation in *avid boating*.

As with bass anglers, trout anglers who purchase books and magazines pertaining to fishing are significantly more likely to participate in both *some boating* and *avid boating*. Unlike bass anglers, however, the impact on the probability of *some boating* and *avid boating* are different, as evidenced by the different coefficients, 0.242 and 0.644.

Trout anglers who also hunted for turkey are significantly less likely to participate in *some boating*, but they are not significantly less likely to participate in *avid boating*.

Similar to bass anglers, trout anglers pursuing some other species have significant differences in their probability of boating participation. Trout anglers who also pursue crappie, striped bass, and freshwater salmon are significantly more likely to participate in *some boating* and *avid boating*. Those who fished for walleye are significantly more likely to participate in *some boating* but not *avid boating*, while those who fished for pike and other freshwater species are not significantly more likely to participate in *some boating*, but given that they do boat, they are significantly more likely to be *avid boaters*.

The results suggest that trout anglers who fish and hunt for numerous different species are more likely to participate in boating. As the number of different species pursued by trout anglers increase, the probability that they will participate in *some boating* increases significantly, which suggests that trout anglers with diverse fishing interests are more likely to participate in boating. This could be because trout anglers who fish for numerous species are more likely to fish for trout in lakes rather than rivers, and boating is more likely for lake fishing. Interestingly, this variable was tested in the bass angler regressions; and, while not significant, it suggested a negative relationship with boating participation. A negative relationship indicates that bass anglers who seek fewer different fish species are more likely to participate in boating.

Trout anglers who hunt numerous different species of animals are significantly more likely to participate in both *some boating* and *avid boating* than those who hunt few species. This could result because hunters who hunt numerous species are likely to be more avid outdoor recreationists, and avid outdoor recreationists are likely to be avid anglers as well.

Table A-3. Analysis of Maximum Likelihood Estimates for Trout Anglers

Parameter	Value	No Boating to Some Boating			Some Boating to Avid Boating		
		Estimate	Chi-Square	Pr > ChiSq	Estimate	Chi-Square	Pr > ChiSq
Intercept		−1.367	49.314	<.0001	−1.918	28.721	<.0001
INCOME		0.056	12.294	0.001	−0.033	1.364	0.243
AGE		0.007	7.237	0.007	0.006	1.396	0.238
CL_TROUT	Two	−0.327	9.337	0.002	−0.158	0.605	0.437
CL_TROUT	Three	0.112	0.592	0.442	0.201	0.721	0.396
CL_TROUT	Four	−0.832	39.842	<.0001	−1.015	9.311	0.002
CL_TROUT	Five	0.493	15.663	<.0001	0.107	0.287	0.592
CL_TROUT	Six	1.034	14.577	0.000	0.322	1.039	0.308
SEX	Female	0.012	0.015	0.901	−0.357	3.165	0.075
MSA	1,000,000 or more	0.063	0.422	0.516	−0.224	1.693	0.193
MSA	250,000–999,999	0.187	2.374	0.123	−0.501	5.027	0.025
MSA	50,000–249,999	−0.023	0.028	0.867	−0.668	6.924	0.009
FISHBOOK	Purchased	0.242	4.009	0.045	0.644	12.644	0.000
TURKEY	Hunted	−0.390	3.926	0.048	−0.109	0.144	0.705
CRAPPIE	Fished	0.472	8.386	0.004	0.896	18.399	<.0001
STRIPED	Fished	0.441	8.462	0.004	0.452	4.675	0.031
WALLEYE	Fished	0.741	17.414	<.0001	0.198	0.751	0.386
PIKE	Fished	0.197	1.070	0.301	0.960	17.736	<.0001
SALMON_F	Fished	0.715	27.914	<.0001	0.413	4.977	0.026
OTHER	Fished	0.246	1.667	0.197	0.698	8.532	0.004
FISHCOUNT		0.138	12.043	0.001	0.013	0.055	0.815
HUNTCOUNT		0.149	27.408	<.0001	0.136	12.116	0.001

U.S. Fish & Wildlife Service
Division of Federal Assistance
Washington, DC 20240

August 2005

www.ingramcontent.com/pod-product-compliance
Lightning Source LLC
Chambersburg PA
CBHW081136280526
45787CB00007B/3107